NYC CHRISTMAS

NEW YORK CHRISTMAS TRAVEL GUIDE

2023

A Pocket Guide Magic of NYC: The Christmas Spectacle - Explore, Experience, and Enjoy.

MICHAEL E. HOWELL

NYC CHRISTMAS

All rights reserved.

No part of this publication may be reproduced, distributed, or transmitted in any form or by any means, including photocopying, recording, or other electronic or mechanical methods, without the prior written permission of the publisher, except for brief quotations embodied in critical reviews and other noncommercial uses permitted by copyright law.

Copyright © 2023 by **MICHAEL E. HOWELL**.

NYC CHRISTMAS

Experience New York City's enchanted wonderland during the most wonderful season of the year, Christmas. The magic and delight that during the holiday season illuminate the busy streets and nooks of this legendary city are yours to immerse with the help of this guide. In New York, Christmas is a show, a holiday that embraces the city with warmth and cheer. Giant Christmas trees stand tall and proud, and the streets are lined with sparkling lights. The air is also filled with laughter and the aroma of cinnamon.

Using this guide will make navigating the city's festive appeal a joyous and stress-free experience. You are invited to feel the enchantment that New York City experiences over the Christmas season by exploring the essence of this magnificent season, which we have carefully chosen. Picture yourself turning the pages while skating at the Rockefeller Center, enjoying hot chocolate at a crowded

NYC CHRISTMAS

winter market, or ambling around streets festooned with holiday lights. Allow yourself to be carried away to a place where happiness knows no boundaries and the Christmas spirit permeates everyone's soul. May this guide serve as an inspiration for you to make treasured memories, laugh with loved ones, and enjoy the real spirit of the holiday season. Allow the Christmastime charm of New York City to infuse your spirit and leave you with a lifetime of unforgettable memories.

A happy and lovely Christmas season to you from the heart of New York City.

NYC CHRISTMAS

CONTENTS

A JOYFUL TALE ABOUT THE MAGIC OF NYC AT CHRISTMAS 8

PREPARING FOR YOUR NYC HOLIDAY ADVENTURE: ADVICE FOR HAVING A GREAT TIME 11

MUST-SEE CHRISTMAS WONDERS 15

    The Christmas Tree At Rockefeller Center: A Colossal Tradition. 15

    Holiday Markets & Shopping: Gifts and Goodies Galore 17

    Ice Skating Rinks: Glide into the Festive Spirit 32

    Stunning Window Displays: A Visual Delight 43

    Christmas in New York City: Festive Shows and Performances: A True Entertainment 55

CREATING YOUR CHRISTMAS ITINERARY 74

    One-Day Christmas Blitz: Make Every Moment Count 74

    Holiday Getaway for Two Days: Double the Joy 78

NYC CHRISTMAS

    Fun Christmas Activities for the Whole Family   83

    Romantic Christmas Escape: Love in the air   92

    NYC Christmas on a Budget: Have Fun Without Breaking the Bank   100

EXPLORING CHRISTMAS DELIGHTS IN NYC   105

    A Visual Feast of the Best Neighborhoods for Holiday Decorations   105

    Delicious Christmas food and treats: Experience the Season   111

    Top NYC Restaurant Picks for a Cozy Christmas Meal: Warming Restaurants   113

    Family-Friendly Christmas Dining in NYC: A Warm Welcome   119

ACCOMMODATIONS   125

    Christmas Retreats: Luxurious Accommodations in the Heart of NYC   125

    Budget-Friendly Festive Stays: Cozy Retreats in NYC for Christmas   136

NYC CHRISTMAS

PRACTICAL TRAVEL GUIDE INFORMATION — 141

Dressing Right: Navigating New York's Christmas Weather — 141

Navigating New York's Festive Season: Essential Tips for Travelers — 142

Staying Safe in the Big Apple: Emergency Information for Your NYC Trip — 145

NYC CHRISTMAS

A JOYFUL TALE ABOUT THE MAGIC OF NYC AT CHRISTMAS

The joy of the holidays in New York City, a paradise where dreams become true, where joy permeates the air, and where the urban landscape sparkles like a million lights in the night sky. This is the entrancing enchantment of Christmas time in New York City, a sight that uplifts and inspires people of all ages.

Imagine yourself ambling along busy streets lined with brilliant lights, each one glistening with the cheer of the season. As though covered in fairy dust, the city changes into a glittering fantasy that spreads joy throughout every nook and corner. Huge Christmas trees that have been decorated with shiny decorations and ribbons keep watch over the celebrations. The Rockefeller Center Christmas Tree, a majestic symbol of unity and optimism, is irresistible. Its lights move in unison, presenting a tale of joy and cohesion. There is an aura of utter

NYC CHRISTMAS

ecstasy as people from all over the globe congregate here, their faces illuminated with surprise and wonder. The attraction of the festive markets is also hard to resist. Unique goods, handcrafted items, and delectable delicacies are found in the rows of beautiful vendors. Warm pretzels and roasted chestnuts flood the air, enveloping you in a cozy, holiday embrace. It's a haven for anyone looking for the ideal present or just wishing to take in the lovely atmosphere.

What fun it is to skate! There are several rinks in the city where you can choose to create priceless moments with friends and family while gliding smoothly or falling over with laughter. It's a classic NYC Christmas experience to feel the brisk winter air on your cheeks and skate on the gleaming ice. The famous businesses in the city's windows deserve their own story. Each exhibit is a piece of art that brings a dream to reality. You feel amazed and inspired by the stories of pleasure, amazement, and generosity that seem to be spoken in the store

NYC CHRISTMAS

windows. Then there are the celebratory plays and performances, which enliven the atmosphere with laughter and song. The stages of New York City come to life with traditional Christmas performances and contemporary versions, bringing holiday happiness to everyone in attendance. A celebration of love, community, and the pleasure of giving takes place in the center of New York City throughout the holiday season. The city is calling you to participate in its charm, experience its warmth, and make memories that will live on in the fabric of your life at this time.

So, my reader becomes lost in the holiday splendor of New York City. Let the glistening lights lead you through this winter paradise, and let the holiday spirit fill your heart with infinite joy, love, and serenity. Your holidays will be memorable thanks to the charm of Christmas time in New York City.

NYC CHRISTMAS

PREPARING FOR YOUR NYC HOLIDAY ADVENTURE: ADVICE FOR HAVING A GREAT TIME

A voyage to remember is setting off on a Christmas excursion in the pulsating center of New York City during this enchanting season. Let's take a nice stroll over some helpful ideas and methods to make your journey a happy and easy experience as you get ready for your adventure into the center of the festivities.

- New York City will be cold in the winter, but don't let that stop you! Put on many layers of warm clothing, a thick hat, gloves, and sturdy boots. You'll be content and ready to pleasantly tour the city if you keep warm.

- Make a list of the must-visit locations, such as the Christmas markets and the Rockefeller Center Tree. Planning

NYC CHRISTMAS

guarantees you won't miss the holiday's best moments.

- The best time to avoid the rush hour is in the morning. Get there early to enjoy a more tranquil experience and fantastic picture possibilities at well-known locations.

- Enjoy the tastes of the time! Warm pretzels and hot cocoa are just two of the delicious pleasures available in NYC to keep your taste buds happy. Don't pass up the chance to enjoy some traditional Christmas favorites.

- New York City's subway system is an excellent option to go fast. Get a MetroCard for simple and affordable transit. The local method of transportation!

- Staying near to the major attractions will cut down on travel time and allow you to take in the festive mood all day. Stay In the Heart of the Action to accommodate a range of budgets, there are several inviting hotels and lodges.

- Don't forget your smartphone or camera! Wonderful images and memories should be captured by the city lights, decorations, and joyful smiles. Relive the magic anytime you want by capturing it.

- New York City is all about sharing happiness. Make eye contact, introduce yourself, and spread holiday cheer to both tourists and residents. greater giving results in greater receiving.

- Your safety is very vital. Keep your possessions nearby and pay attention to your surroundings. Stay updated about weather predictions and any special events occurring during your stay.

NYC CHRISTMAS

- Finally, welcome the unanticipated. The finest moments sometimes happen unexpectedly. Allow the city to surprise you and be open to new experiences.

Your holiday vacation in New York City is waiting for you, promising amazement and happiness. Follow these easy suggestions, let the enchantment of the season fill your heart, and be ready to enjoy yourself to the fullest in New York City. Travel safely.

NYC CHRISTMAS

MUST-SEE CHRISTMAS WONDERS

The Christmas Tree At Rockefeller Center: A Colossal Tradition.

The Rockefeller Center Christmas Tree is an enormous tree known for its festive charm. It's like the Christmas tree that rules New York City! Every year, when they light up this tree, people become really enthusiastic. It's not just any tree; rather, it's the Christmas season's biggest star.

Imagine a tree that reaches up to the sky, complete with sparkling decorations, shimmering lights, and a large, dazzling star on top. It resembles a huge holiday display in several ways. This unique tree has a rich past. It has been a custom for a very, very long time. For many years, families have traveled to visit this wonderful tree. It serves as a venue for gathering and season's pleasure celebration. And where can you locate this enormous tree? In the

NYC CHRISTMAS

heart of Rockefeller Center in New York City. The Center resembles a large meeting space where people congregate to work, shop, and celebrate the season. The tree is there, in the middle of the city, casting its merry spell on everyone who walks by. So you can't miss viewing this tree if you're in New York City during the holidays. It is a resounding tradition that adds to the Christmas season's sense of awe and pleasure.

NYC CHRISTMAS

Holiday Markets & Shopping: Gifts and Goodies Galore

You definitely have to try entering a festive paradise that is teeming with little booths and businesses, each of which is providing something unique especially for you. A place filled with one-of-a-kind items, tasty delicacies, and exquisite crafts. You'll go through these enchanted markets as you continue reading to experience the utter delight they provide over the Christmas season.

❖ **Union Square GreenMarket:**

A vibrant, busy area tucked away in the center of New York City, where the spirit of the holiday season comes to life. The Union Square GreenMarket is this lively location, and during the Christmas holiday season, it becomes a joyful center. The market is located in Union Square, a popular gathering spot in the city, particularly during the Christmas season. Every year, as

NYC CHRISTMAS

Christmas gets closer, the market decks itself up in seasonal flair and invites residents and guests to share in the joy. Rows of booths, each painted in a cheerful shade and embellished with charming details. Each booth has its personality and is ready and willing to make passersby happy. The market transforms into a paradise of varied offers, infusing the air with an alluring scent and providing everything; fresh vegetables as well as handcrafted crafts and delicious sweets.

The vibe at the Union Square GreenMarket is like being embraced in a cozy hug. As people examine the wares of each booth, there are smiles and warm discussions all around. As shoppers uncover the riches that are waiting for them, laughter and joy reverberate throughout the market. The variety of products on offer is one of this market's noteworthy characteristics. It's plenty of gift suggestions; soft scarves and ornate decorations. Additionally, the aromas of hot chocolate and toasted almonds fill the air and entice your senses. Farmers and craftsmen

NYC CHRISTMAS

come together to display their skills at the Union Square GreenMarket, which personifies a spirit of community. It's a location where you can interact with the artisans, learn about their backgrounds, and sense the love and commitment they put into their works.

The experience, however, extends beyond simple business dealings. It's about becoming fully involved in the celebrations; the fun of exploring the market, finding interesting products, and enjoying happy moments with friends and family. A Christmastime trip to the Union Square GreenMarket is more than just a chance to buy; it's also a chance to experience the beauty of the season. This is where the Christmas season in NYC is enhanced and made to be genuinely unique since the spirit of giving and community shines here.

NYC CHRISTMAS

❖ **Bryant Park Winter Village: A Holiday Wonderland in New York City**

Picture a bright and energetic spot situated within the heart of New York City, where the enchantment of the Christmas season flourishes. This enchanted community adorns Bryant Park, a famous gathering spot in the city, particularly during the holidays. The park decks itself up in seasonal flair as Christmas approaches, inviting residents and guests to celebrate the season.

You will see a row of little shops, each with its distinct charm and decked up in holiday décor. Every vendor is a hidden gem, providing a wide range of goods. Delightful smells fill the air, titillating your senses. At Bryant Park Winter Village, the vibe is one of a cozy embrace. As guests examine the goods at each stand, laughter and upbeat discussions fill the air. As people find the hidden jewels, awe and excitement are evident. The wide variety of options available in this

NYC CHRISTMAS

community is one of its notable features. It's a sanctuary for individuals looking for unique presents, cozy scarves and complex decorations. And speaking of tastes, the air is tantalizingly perfumed with the fragrance of hot chocolate and toasted almonds.

Bryant Park Winter Village is a celebration of the local neighborhood when craftsmen and entrepreneurs get together to show off their work. Here, you can get to know the inventive minds that are responsible for the crafts, hear their tales, and sense the passion they put into what they do. However, the experience goes beyond just business. It's about becoming fully involved in the celebrations, the fun of wandering about the town, finding interesting things, and enjoying yourself with loved ones. Bryant Park Winter Village is a place to appreciate the beauty of the season. It's a location where the Christmas season in NYC is enhanced and made all the more memorable by the genuine sense of giving and community.

NYC CHRISTMAS

- ❖ **Christmas Grand Central Holiday Fair: A Festive Extravaganza**

A lively, crowded location in the center of New York City where the Christmas spirit is dancing in the air. The Grand Central Holiday Fair, a genuine holiday spectacle, is located in this bustling area. PGrand Central Terminal, a busy metropolitan center where people congregate, particularly during the Christmas season, is graced by this colorful market. The station changes into a joyful refuge as Christmas approaches, encouraging residents and tourists to share in the festive happiness.

Imagine a line of charming booths, each displaying a festive display and exhibiting a special product. A piece of someone's heart is kept at each booth, which offers a variety of pleasures including delicious sweets and handmade ornaments. A sensory thrill is promised as the air is infused with pleasant smells. The Grand Central Holiday Fair has a cozy, friendly atmosphere that embraces everyone

NYC CHRISTMAS

who enters. As guests examine the goods at each stand, laughter and upbeat discussions fill the air. As individuals discover hidden riches, awe and enthusiasm are obvious. The variety of products on sale at this fair is one of its best qualities. It's a treasure trove for anyone looking for unique presents, comfortable scarves as well as ornate decorations. The tastes are also a pleasure in and of themselves, with the alluring scent of hot chocolate and toasted almonds.

A celebration of creativity and neighborhood, the Grand Central Holiday Fair brings together makers and artists to display their works. You can meet the creative minds that created these crafts here, hear their tales, and sense the passion they put into what they do. The experience extends beyond simple business dealings. It's about becoming fully involved in the celebrations, the fun of exploring the fair, finding interesting things, and enjoying yourself with loved ones. Christmastime shopping at the Grand Central Holiday Fair is only one aspect

NYC CHRISTMAS

of the invitation to appreciate the enchantment of the season. It's a location where the Christmas season in NYC is enhanced and made all the more memorable by the genuine sense of giving and community.

❖ **Columbus Circle Holiday Market:**

A bustling meeting place where Christmas cheer is in the air, right in the middle of New York City. The Columbus Circle Festive Market, a genuine celebration of the festive season, is this bustling center. In New York City, in Columbus Circle, is where you can find the Columbus Circle Holiday Market. At the southwest corner of Central Park sits Columbus Circle, a well-known and active crossroads. It serves as a focal point for gatherings and a center of activity, particularly during the Christmas season when the market adds a festive air to the neighborhood.

NYC CHRISTMAS

Columbus Circle is graced by this beautiful market. The neighborhood changes into a joyful refuge as Christmas draws near, inviting both residents and guests to join in the festive fun. Imagine a stretch of charming booths, each presenting its distinctive goods and decked up in festive decorations. Every vendor's stand exudes the enthusiasm of its maker and offers a variety of pleasures. A sensory adventure is promised by the lovely fragrances permeating the air.

The Columbus Circle Holiday Market has a welcoming, pleasant ambiance that envelops everyone in a loving hug. As guests examine the goods at each stand, laughter and upbeat discussions fill the air. As individuals discover hidden riches, awe and enthusiasm are obvious. The range of options offered is one of this market's noteworthy characteristics. It's a treasure trove for anyone looking for unique presents. And, the tastes are a feast for the senses, especially the alluring scent of hot chocolate and toasted almonds. At the

NYC CHRISTMAS

Columbus Circle Holiday Market, artists, creators, and members of the community come together to share their skills and celebrate creativity. Here, you can decide to get to know the creative brains behind the crafts, hear their tales, and sense the passion they have for what they do. The experience goes beyond simple shopping. It's about becoming fully involved in the celebrations, the fun of exploring the market, finding interesting products, and enjoying yourself with loved ones.

An invitation to enjoy the charm of the season is extended when one visits the Columbus Circle Holiday Market during the Christmas season. It's a location where the Christmas season in NYC is enhanced and made all the more memorable by the genuine sense of giving and community.

❖ **Chelsea Market: A Joyous Haven**

A bustling, energetic location in the center of New York City where the Christmas spirit is contagious.

NYC CHRISTMAS

This vibrant market adorns the Chelsea district, a thriving downtown neighborhood where people congregate, particularly during the Christmas season. As Christmas draws near, the market changes into a joyful setting that welcomes both residents and guests to partake in the festivities. The Chelsea area of Manhattan, New York City, is home to the Chelsea Market.

Its precise location is 75 Ninth Avenue, which is located between 15th and 16th Streets. This thriving neighborhood is renowned for its upbeat ambiance, variety of dining choices, distinctive stores, and active community. The market is a well-liked hangout for residents and visitors looking for a wide variety of dining and shopping experiences since it is conveniently located. Imagine a collection of adorable booths, each showcasing a different product and decked up in festive décor. Offering a variety of pleasures, each station has a unique tale to tell. A wonderful sensory experience is promised by the lovely fragrances that permeate the air.

NYC CHRISTMAS

Chelsea Market has a cozy, welcoming atmosphere throughout the holiday season that extends a warm welcome to everybody. As guests examine the goods at each stand, laughter and upbeat discussions fill the air. As individuals uncover buried riches, awe and enthusiasm are obvious. The wide variety of options available in this sector is one of its notable features.

It's a treasure trove for anyone looking for unique presents, comfortable scarves and ornate decorations. Additionally, the tastes are a feast for the senses, especially the alluring scent of hot chocolate and toasted almonds. When it comes to holiday shopping, going to Chelsea Market is more of an invitation to immerse yourself in the beauty of the season. It's a location where the Christmas season in NYC is enhanced and made all the more memorable by the genuine sense of giving and community.

NYC CHRISTMAS

- ❖ **Fifth Avenue Shops: New York City's Festive Wonderland**

A festive and upbeat area in the center of New York City, when the season is in full swing. Fifth Avenue is a bustling area that is a Christmastime beacon of festivity. One of the principal avenues in New York City, Fifth Avenue passes through the borough of Manhattan. The stores and boutiques are situated along Fifth Avenue, which runs from Greenwich Village's Washington Square Park in the south up to Harlem's 143rd Street in the north.

Midtown Manhattan is where you'll find the majority of the prominent merchants, premium brands, and flagship stores. This neighborhood is known for its high-end shopping and landmark businesses. It's a popular retail area in NYC that draws both residents and visitors, particularly during the joyous holiday season. It is well-known for its beautiful Christmas decorations and frenzied bustle. The avenue decks itself up in seasonal flair

NYC CHRISTMAS

as Christmas draws near, enticing residents and tourists to join in the fun. A row of elegant stores, each presenting its distinctive goods with bright lights and wonderful décor. As guests go by and take in the festive atmosphere, a feeling of amazement permeates the air. Christmastime on Fifth Avenue has a cozy, welcoming ambiance that embraces everyone in a loving hug. As customers peruse the merchandise at each store, laughter and happiness are heard everywhere. As individuals unearth hidden gems and locate the ideal presents for their loved ones, a spirit of surprise and excitement permeates the area.

The grandeur of Fifth Avenue's offerings is one of its noteworthy characteristics. It's a treasure trove for individuals looking for unique presents. The decorations are a visual feast and a reflection of the festive mood in the air. People from all walks of life congregate on Fifth Avenue throughout the holiday season to partake in the festivities. It's a location where the Christmas season in NYC is enhanced

NYC CHRISTMAS

and made all the more memorable by the genuine sense of giving and community.

Going to these places during the holidays is like stepping into a joyful wonderland. There are so many things to see, taste, and discover. It's a shopping adventure, and each market is like a new chapter in a festive story.

NYC CHRISTMAS

Ice Skating Rinks: Glide into the Festive Spirit

Visualize yourself skating through a smooth, frozen playground while wearing ice skates. It's not just an ordinary glide; this glide evokes the excitement of the season. Ice skating rinks are the names for these frozen areas. Entering the ice feels like stepping into a winter paradise. People of various ages are spinning and swirling while dressed warmly. The delight of the brisk wind on your face fills the air with laughter.

A location where the people are warm and smiling, even when the earth is freezing. These ice skating rinks are precisely that; a blend of holiday cheer and winter enchantment. There is a certain sort of delight that comes with gliding on the ice, regardless of your skill level or if this is your first time. These rinks become more than simply skating surfaces over the holidays. They develop into a center for joy and festivity. Lights flash, and sometimes music is heard playing in the background. It's a location where friends and family go to take in the pure joy of skating. So, when you see ice skating rinks, picture yourself entering a realm where the atmosphere is joyfully festive and the ice is your dance floor. It's a happy gliding into the holiday mood that leaves you with flushed cheeks and a heart full of delight.

❖ **The Rink at Rockefeller Center:**

A lively, crowded spot in the center of New York City where the winter wonderland comes to life on the ice. The Rink at Rockefeller Center is this energetic location; during Christmas, it becomes like a winter wonderland. The Rink at Rockefeller Center is situated in Midtown Manhattan at 600 Fifth Avenue, a busy junction. It is located within the legendary Rockefeller Center, a recognized emblem of the city known for its tall towers. There is a smooth, frozen surface surrounded by tall structures that are decked up in holiday lights and

NYC CHRISTMAS

decorations. Skaters of all ages smoothly move over the ice while beaming grins. Laughter and the cheery sounds of festive music permeate the air. Christmastime at The Rink at Rockefeller Center is comfortable and welcoming, encasing everyone in a warm hug. Families, groups of friends, and even lone skaters gather to celebrate the festive season.

This rink's beautiful backdrop; the imposing Rockefeller Center Christmas Tree; is one of its most outstanding attractions. Towering above the ice, it is a sight to see. It is decked with tens of thousands of flashing lights, and on top is a gorgeous star. Christmastime skating at The Rink at Rockefeller Center is a tradition. People get together and enjoy the enchantment of the Christmas season this way. It's a location where the fun of skating and the magic of Christmas come together to create lifelong memories.

NYC CHRISTMAS

❖ **Wollman Rink in Central Park:**

A lively, crowded area in the center of New York City where the energy of the season is permeating the ice. Wollman Rink is this lively area, and during the holidays it is a great skating haven. Wollman Rink is located in Central Park, a refuge of greenery among the bustle of the city. The location is in the southeast corner of Central Park and has the address 830 Fifth Avenue.

It is in a fantastic position that is both convenient and popular with both residents and tourists. A sparkling, frozen lake surrounded by the breathtaking scenery of the park and the skyline of the city. All ages of skaters go gracefully over the ice as applause and joy fill the brisk air. It's the ideal location for both romantic getaways and family trips because of the loving atmosphere. Wollman Rink has a warm and welcoming ambiance during Christmas. Couples enjoy a romantic spin on the ice, families create precious moments, and friends get together. It consists of a mixture of laughing, conversation, and the pure pleasure of skating. This rink's location in Central Park is one of its charming attractions. The city's skyscrapers on one side and the serene, unspoiled beauty of the park on the other make skating here a special experience. Christmas skating at Wollman Rink is about getting into the holiday mood. It's a happy custom that many people participate in to usher in the Christmas season. It's a spot where children's joy and skaters' spins combine to form a magical symphony that echoes Christmas cheer.

❖ **Bryant Park Winter Village Ice Rink:**

A busy, energetic area in the center of New York City where the holiday season elevates the commonplace to the spectacular. Bryant Park Winter Village Ice Rink; a wonderful skating hideaway over the holidays. At a busy intersection in Midtown Manhattan, 40th Street and Sixth Avenue, is where you'll find the Bryant Park Winter

NYC CHRISTMAS

Village Ice Rink. It is a major core of celebrations and excitement that is conveniently located inside Bryant Park and open to anyone. A dazzling, icy sanctuary tucked between soaring skyscrapers and sparkling streetlights. Skaters glide over the ice while wearing warm clothing, their smiles and joy filling the brisk winter air.

People congregate there to celebrate the pleasure of the holiday season. During the Christmas season, Bryant Park Winter Village Ice Rink has a welcoming ambience. Friends congregate there for happy skating sessions, and families make priceless memories there. It consists of a mixture of laughing, conversation, and the pure pleasure of skating. The setting of this rink is one of its appealing qualities. A winter paradise is created in Bryant Park, with vendors selling food, gifts, and crafts. It's the ideal place to relax, have some hot chocolate, and take in the holiday spirit. Christmas skating at Bryant Park Winter Village Ice Rink is more than simply skating; it's about getting into the holiday mood. It's

NYC CHRISTMAS

an annual custom to escape into a happy world. It's a location where the festive spirit comes alive on the ice, leaving you with pleasant feelings and priceless memories.

- ❖ **Lasker Rink in Central Park:**

A tranquil, snowy sanctuary tucked away in the middle of New York City, where the spirit of the season elegantly permeates the atmosphere. Lasker Rink is located in Central Park's northern region, notably close to Lenox Avenue and 110th Street. It provides a fantastic getaway for both residents and tourists since it is a tranquil refuge within the city's hustle and bustle.

Visualize a frozen body of water surrounded by trees and Central Park's serene beauty. Skaters of all ages glide over the ice while beaming grins. The sounds of pleasure and laughing fill the chilly air, creating a festive chorus. Lasker Rink has a warm and welcoming ambiance during Christmas.

NYC CHRISTMAS

Families congregate, friends get together, and people pause to breathe in the serene atmosphere. It combines friendship, happiness, and the simple pleasure of skating on ice. The location of this rink in Central Park is one of its amazing qualities. In the middle of the city's grandeur, skating here gives a special connection to nature. The neighboring woods, which are often covered in snow, provide skaters a beautiful background.

Christmastime skating at Lasker Rink is an embracing of the season. Many people follow this custom as a way to mark the occasion and generate priceless memories. A feeling of calm and the enchantment of the holidays fill your heart as you experience the thrill of skating in harmony with the quiet of nature there.

❖ **Sky Rink at Chelsea Piers:**

A bustling, happy place in the center of New York City where the holiday spirit is palpable. The Sky

NYC CHRISTMAS

Rink at Chelsea Piers is a lively location and a popular place to ice skate during the holidays. Within Chelsea Piers, a thriving sports facility along the Hudson River sits Sky Rink. Its position in Manhattan is convenient and well-liked by both residents and tourists. Its address is 61 Chelsea Piers.

Visualize entering a big ice rink and being enveloped by a metropolis and the river beyond. Skaters of all abilities glide over the ice with ease; the enthusiasm is palpable. There is a vibrant environment created by laughter and companionship. Christmastime at Sky Rink has a warm, contagious atmosphere. Families gather together, friends have fun, and people enjoy the excitement of skating. It combines delight, special times with others, and the pure thrill of skating. This rink's indoor location is one of its unique qualities. Here, skating provides a cozy setting that is protected from the winter cold while retaining the same feeling of pleasure and freedom.

NYC CHRISTMAS

❖ **LeFrak Center at Lakeside, Prospect Park:**

During the holiday season, LeFrak Center at Lakeside, Prospect Park offers festive skating in New York City. A bustling, joyous location where the Christmas season comes alive, right in the middle of Brooklyn, New York. At 171 East Drive, the LeFrak Center at Lakeside is tucked away in Brooklyn's expansive Prospect Park.

It's a lovely area that's simple for everyone to get to, drawing both residents and tourists, particularly around the holidays. Skaters of various ages and abilities smoothly glide over the ice as their pleasure and laughter fill the brisk winter air. The neighborhood comes together to enjoy the spirit of the holidays there. Christmastime at the LeFrak Center is warm and welcoming, fostering a feeling of community and celebration. Families gather together, friends share special moments, and many

NYC CHRISTMAS

just enjoy skating. It combines fun, friendship, and the sheer joy of skating on ice. This rink's unique qualities include its lovely location inside Prospect Park. Here, skating offers a unique experience that seamlessly combines urban life with scenic beauty. A deeper experience of the festive mood should be had by skating at the LeFrak Center throughout the Christmas season. It's a custom that helps people have memorable holiday experiences. It's a location where the fun of skating and the holiday cheer converge, leaving you with a heart full of warmth and memories.

NYC CHRISTMAS

Stunning Window Displays: A Visual Delight

Beautiful Christmas window displays in New York City are a visual feast. During the Christmas holiday when strolling through city streets that are lined with eye-catching storefront displays. These exhibits have been thoughtfully created to make you feel festive. You will feel the enchantment of Christmas right in the middle of the city thanks to the combination of these displays. Listed down are some places in New York City known for their stunning window displays during Christmas:

❖ **Saks Fifth Avenue:**

A bustling neighborhood in the heart of New York City during the holiday season, when breathtaking sights bring the enchantment of Christmas to life. Saks Fifth Avenue is a bustling location that epitomizes luxury and ingenuity around Christmas.

NYC CHRISTMAS

At 611 Fifth Avenue, a busy intersection in Midtown Manhattan, you will find Saks Fifth Avenue. Its central location, made possible by the address, makes it a must-see location, particularly during the Christmas season. You will witness a great display of creativity in the windows of Saks Fifth Avenue while strolling along a busy street. The decorations are meticulously made, and each one tells a special tale that captures the spirit of the season. Crowds are attracted, and they are in awe of the workmanship and attention to detail.

Christmastime brings a feeling of wonder and enthusiasm to the area surrounding Saks Fifth Avenue. Families, groups of friends, and even lone travelers congregate to see the magnificent show being played out via the window displays. Exclamations of excitement and awe flood the air, making the atmosphere vibrant and joyful. The shared experience is what gives Saks Fifth Avenue's displays their enchantment rather than simply the aesthetic appeal. The goal is to unite people and

NYC CHRISTMAS

immerse them in the magic of the season. The decorations showcase the city's vivacious character and enthusiasm for extravagant and artistic Christmas celebrations. It's an invitation to enter a world of creativity and imagination to visit Saks Fifth Avenue throughout the holiday season. You'll come away from it with treasured memories and a heart full of festive cheer. It's an opportunity to disappear into a visual paradise.

❖ **Bergdorf Goodman Christmas Displays:**

A busy neighborhood in New York City during the holidays where creativity is brought to life by stunning visuals. In the heart of Midtown Manhattan, at 754 Fifth Avenue, is the site of Bergdorf Goodman. It encourages everyone to watch a great display of richness and craftsmanship because of its prominent location, especially during the holiday season. Visualize yourself traveling down Fifth Avenue and coming across Bergdorf Goodman's opulent window displays. Each exhibit

NYC CHRISTMAS

is a work of art that has been thoughtfully chosen to tell the story of the holidays. The audience is captivated and transported into a realm of elegance and beauty by the amazing workmanship and attention to detail.

During Christmas, there is a sophisticated and magical atmosphere. Shoppers and onlookers congregate to see the artwork displayed in the windows. An atmosphere of festivity is created by the appreciation and Christmas happiness that permeate the air. The exhibits at Bergdorf Goodman are captivating not just for their aesthetic value but also for the experiences they provide. It's an invitation to lose oneself in a world of luxury and imagination, where the festive spirit is captured in art and design. These decorations showcase the city's appreciation of the opulent and exquisite, making it a sought-after vacation spot around Christmas.

NYC CHRISTMAS

❖ Tiffany & Co.:

There is this quaint and energetic neighborhood in New York City around the holidays, when grace and elegance cover the streets. This charming location is Tiffany & Co., a real display of luxury over the holidays. In a prominent Midtown Manhattan site at 727 Fifth Avenue, Tiffany & Co. is housed. Due to its convenient location and magnificent display of elegance, it draws many visitors, particularly during the Christmas season.

Stroll down Fifth Avenue and stop to admire Tiffany & Co.'s beautiful window displays. Each window is a unique piece of art that has been painstakingly created to capture the spirit of the season. Viewers are in awe of the superb workmanship and attention to detail. Christmastime is a time of refinement and awe all over Tiffany & Co. Visitors and bystanders congregate to savor the enduring beauty shown in the windows. An atmosphere of elegance and refinement is created

NYC CHRISTMAS

by the appreciation and joy that permeate the air. The appeal of Tiffany & Co.'s exhibitions goes beyond aesthetic appeal; it's an adventure. It's an invitation to enter a world of refinement and luxury, where the spirit of the season is captured in exquisite design. These exhibits reflect the city's love for elegance and beauty, making it a popular holiday destination. The confluence of art and festivity is witnessed while visiting Tiffany & Co. during Christmas. It's a chance to take part in a visual feast that honors the time of year and makes an impact.

❖ **Macy's Herald Square:**

A busy and energetic center during the holidays in New York City, where the Christmas spirit is brought to life by eye-catching decorations. In the heart of Midtown Manhattan, at 151 West 34th Street, is where you'll find Macy's Herald Square. Its advantageous location makes it simple to get to, encouraging everyone to enjoy the splendor of the

NYC CHRISTMAS

season with its enormous displays. When entering Macy's Herald Square, you will be welcomed by the lively and captivating window displays as you stroll through the busy streets. Each exhibit is expertly constructed, bringing the wonder and pleasure of Christmas to life. Viewers are in awe of the ingenuity and meticulous attention to detail. Around Christmas, there is an air of surprise and excitement.

Tourists, friends, and families congregate to ogle the magnificent displays. A joyful and festive atmosphere is created by the cheers and holiday mirth that fill the air. The attractiveness of Macy's exhibits in Herald Square lies not just in their aesthetic appeal but also in the feelings they arouse. It is a call to enter a world of celebration and wonder where the enchantment of Christmas is exquisitely captured via imaginative storytelling. Due to these exhibits, the city becomes a well-liked holiday destination throughout the holiday season.

NYC CHRISTMAS

A Christmas visit to Macy's Herald Square is an invitation to savor the festive atmosphere. It's an opportunity to experience the Christmas season's unique combination of creativity and celebration, which makes a lasting impression on the soul.

❖ **Bloomingdale's:**

A vibrant and busy neighborhood in New York City during the holiday season, when energy and enthusiasm brighten the area. In terms of holiday cheer, Bloomingdale's is the quintessential location. In the Upper East Side of Manhattan, at 1000 Third Avenue, Bloomingdale's is situated in a convenient and central location. Particularly during the holiday season, its location makes it a lovely destination for visitors looking for a combination of style and Christmas charm. Visualize yourself wandering along the bustling streets and coming across Bloomingdale's' vibrant and themed window displays. Each exhibit is thoughtfully created to convey a different Christmas tale. The creative flare

NYC CHRISTMAS

and meticulous attention to detail captivate viewers and leave them in awe. Shoppers and onlookers congregate to see the creativity shown in the windows. A dynamic and festive environment is created by the adoration and festive delight that permeate the air.

Bloomingdale's displays have a fascination that goes beyond just aesthetic appeal; it's an experience. It's an invitation to immerse oneself in a festive, creative environment where the true spirit of the season is beautifully captured. The city's penchant for fusing flair with festivity is reflected in these decorations, which make it a sought-after vacation spot during Christmas. Christmastime offers the opportunity to experience a mix of creativity and celebration at Bloomingdale's. It's an opportunity to take part in an unforgettable visual experience that honors the season.

NYC CHRISTMAS

❖ Barneys New York:

A vibrant and busy area of New York City around the holidays, when creativity and art are shown everywhere. At 660 Madison Avenue, on Manhattan's Upper East Side, Is where you will find Barneys New York. Because of its advantageous location, it is a center for creative exhibits and draws tourists from all around.

You will admire Barneys New York's innovative and contemporary window displays while strolling along Madison Avenue. Each exhibit is a work of art that has been painstakingly created to capture the spirit of the occasion. Onlookers are astounded by the extraordinary ingenuity and attention to detail. Around Barneys New York during Christmas, there is a sense of awe and admiration for the arts. Locals, visitors, and art aficionados congregate to ogle the cutting-edge exhibits. The atmosphere is one of creative celebration as there is a palpable feeling of appreciation and festive cheer. Barneys New York

NYC CHRISTMAS

displays are captivating not just for their aesthetic appeal but also for the feelings they arouse. The spirit of Christmas is reinterpreted in contemporary manifestations, and it's an invitation to immerse oneself in a world of modern inventiveness and seasonal pleasure. These exhibits reflect the city's appreciation of creativity and innovation, making it a popular holiday destination.

❖ **Lord & Taylor:**

A positively-charged neighborhood in New York City where the streets are adorned with elegance and tradition. Lord & Taylor is a beautiful place that embodies the beauty of the holidays around Christmas. At Midtown Manhattan, at 424 Fifth Avenue, Lord & Taylor is situated there at a convenient and central location. During Christmas when you stop to admire Lord & Taylor's elegant and charming window displays. Each display is a unique piece of art that has been painstakingly created to capture the wonder and pleasure of

NYC CHRISTMAS

Christmas. The workmanship and meticulous attention to detail astonish onlookers. There is a sophisticated and nostalgic atmosphere. Visitors and shoppers congregate to see the elegance and beauty shown in the windows. An atmosphere of beautiful celebration is created by the adoration and festive happiness that permeate the air.

Lord & Taylor's window displays are alluring for more reasons than just their aesthetic value. It's a warm invitation to enter a world of elegance and grace, where the true spirit of the season is exquisitely captured. These decorations showcase the city's appreciation for elegance and history, making it a popular holiday trip. Giving yourself a trip to Lord & Taylor at Christmas gives you the chance to experience a fusion of classic beauty and holiday cheer. It's an opportunity to immerse oneself in a memorable experience that honors the holiday.

NYC CHRISTMAS

Christmas in New York City: Festive Shows and Performances: A True Entertainment

The crowded streets of New York City during the cheery holiday season, when there is a palpable sense of expectation in the air. This is the time of year when the city comes to life with a wide variety of performances and events, enhancing the holiday spirit with a unique type of enchantment. Below are some places in New York known for their festive shows and performances during Christmas:

❖ **Radio City Music Hall:**

Christmas at Radio City Music Hall is a lavish holiday spectacle in New York City. A festive atmosphere and a humming of expectation. The setting for this charming scenario is Radio City Music Hall, which around Christmas is the pinnacle of opulence and entertainment. In the heart of Midtown Manhattan, at 1260 Avenue of the

NYC CHRISTMAS

Americas, Radio City Music Hall dominates the landscape. Both residents and tourists are drawn to it by its towering presence. You are invited inside by the festively decorated tent, which creates the right atmosphere for what is within. You are welcomed inside by a sight of happiness and creativity. The Rockettes Christmas Spectacular takes place on stage, and for many people, it has become a holiday ritual.

During the holiday season, Radio City Music Hall is nothing short of amazing. The audience is transported to a paradise by the interior's lighting and décor. You are instantly transported to a world of pure festive joy by the music, dancing, and vivid costumes. Precision dancers known as The Rockettes captivate the audience with their flawless performances and contagious pleasure. Everyone in attendance grins as a result of the synchronicity and zeal in their performance, which also leaves everyone with fond recollections. Radio City Music Hall is an experience that captures the pure spirit of

NYC CHRISTMAS

Christmas. Families, friends, and lone travelers congregate there to enjoy the festive season and take in a show that makes them feel the beauty of the season.

❖ **Lincoln Center:**

Think of the jovial Christmas vibe that permeates New York City. Lincoln Center, the pinnacle of holiday joy and ethnic diversity, sits in the heart of this revelry. Located at 10 Lincoln Center Plaza on Manhattan's Upper West Side, Lincoln Center emerges during this festive season as a light for the arts and entertainment. You are met with Lincoln Center's majesty as you approach it. A magical scene is created by the center's lights and gorgeous architecture. It's a location where celebrations and creativity coexist together. During the Christmas season, Lincoln Center has a lively and energizing ambiance. The uplifting music of concerts, the beautiful dances of ballets, and the enchantment of musicals bring the halls to life. The many performances capture the magic and delight of the season. Lincoln Center looks to be filled with festive spirit in every nook and cranny. To participate in this cultural spectacle, people of all ages and origins join together. An exquisite tapestry of holiday memories is created through the shared experience of art and performance. Lincoln Center provides a fostering environment for the festive spirit in addition to being a center for the arts. Families, friends, and people congregate there to enjoy the diversity of the culture and the festivities. One is invited to be delighted by the performing arts by going to Lincoln Center over the holidays. It's an opportunity to see a mix of creative styles that characterize the Christmas season.

❖ **The Apollo Theater:**

In Harlem, a hub of culture in the core of Manhattan, at 253 West 125th Street, sits the Apollo Theater with pride. Due to its position, it serves as a hub for those looking for exciting holiday activities.

NYC CHRISTMAS

You are instantly attracted to The Apollo Theater by its recognizable marquee, which is lit up for the holidays. It's a warm sight that suggests visitors will have a good time there. Christmas cheer is in the air. You are greeted inside by the sounds of enthusiastic entertainment. The theater comes to life with entertaining concerts and performances that reflect the holiday cheer. The stage serves as a blank canvas for musical celebrations and creative expression.

The Apollo Theater has a festive environment that is energizing. The show's rhythm and spirit captivate the crowd, which is made up of both regulars and newcomers. An atmosphere of group celebration is created by the laughter, applause, and shouts that are heard everywhere. The Apollo Theater is a bustling center where people congregate to enjoy the festivities. It's a location where generations interact and exchange memories that last a lifetime. Christmastime at The Apollo Theater is an invitation to join in on a festive

NYC CHRISTMAS

celebration. It's an opportunity to take in performances that personify the spirit of the season and leave you feeling warmed within by the delight of the occasion.

❖ **Broadway Theaters:**

Numerous theaters along Broadway present special Christmas-themed performances and musicals, adding to the festive cheer. Listed down are famous active Broadway theaters during Christmas:

- **Winter Garden Theatre:**

The Winter Garden Theatre, located at 1634 Broadway in the center of Midtown Manhattan, is a center for entertainment and innovation. Those seeking Broadway's festive enchantment will simply get it because of its convenient location. As you get closer to the Winter Garden Theatre, you're greeted by its recognizable marquee, which is decked up in lights and holiday décor. It's an invitation to enter a magical and wonder-filled

NYC CHRISTMAS

universe. The Winter Garden Theatre's holiday atmosphere is nothing short of amazing. The energy of the performances animates the elegantly decorated space. The audience is enthralled by the spirit of the season as the theater transforms into a world where tales are told. Young and elderly audiences alike congregate to see the magic that adorns the Winter Garden Theatre. The joint enjoyment of live performance becomes a treasured memory for everyone. It's a place where people's hearts are touched, and the festive cheer lasts long after the show is over.

- **New Amsterdam Theatre:**

Steeped in history and elegance, it hosts enthralling shows that draw audiences seeking the magic of Christmas. The New Amsterdam Theatre is a beacon of entertainment and creative delight located at 214 West 42nd Street in the busy Times Square. Due to its convenient location, everyone is encouraged to enjoy Broadway throughout the holiday celebrations. As you get closer to the New

NYC CHRISTMAS

Amsterdam Theatre, you can't help but be drawn in by its distinctive marquee, which exudes a classic appeal and conjures the long history of Broadway. It's an invitation to enter a universe where the possibilities are endless. You are immediately taken to an enchanted world of dramatic beauty as soon as you arrive. The New Amsterdam Theatre's holiday atmosphere is nothing short of wonderful. The interiors reflect the artistic talent that adorns the stage with their lavish décor and minute touches. With stories that warm hearts and enliven the festive spirit, the performances come alive in the spirit of the occasion. At the New Amsterdam Theatre, friends, family, and theater lovers congregate to see the magic develop on stage. Live performances foster a feeling of community and increase the festive spirit of the season.

- **St. James Theatre:**

A Broadway classic, presenting holiday-themed performances that embrace the spirit of the season, delighting theater enthusiasts. The St. James

NYC CHRISTMAS

Theatre offers a fantastic position at 246 West 44th Street in the thriving Theater District, drawing theatergoers looking for the festive enchantment of Broadway. You are welcomed with its vintage marquee, a beloved landmark in the busy downtown. The theater's charm evokes a bygone age and is evocative of Broadway's illustrious past. As soon as you enter, the atmosphere of the season is immediately evoked by the performances that take place there.

The St. James Theatre has a joyful and energizing Christmastime atmosphere. The loud music and energetic performances fill the venues. It's a location where the pleasure of the holidays magnifies the wonder of live entertainment. Theater lovers go to the St. James Theatre to appreciate the art of the stage. Families, friends, and tourists assemble here to take part in the enchantment as it happens and leave with priceless holiday memories.

NYC CHRISTMAS

- **Minskoff Theatre:**

With its grand ambiance, it hosts special Christmas performances, bringing the magic of Broadway to life during the holidays. The Minskoff Theatre is prominently situated at 200 West 45th Street in the center of Times Square, encouraging everyone to enjoy the wonder of Broadway throughout the joyous celebrations.

The Minskoff Theatre's imposing marquee catches your eye as you go closer. It promises to take you on a trip into a realm where imagination reigns supreme. The Minskoff Theatre has a magical ambience over the holidays. The elegant and refined interiors serve as the ideal setting for the stunning performances. The holiday-themed performances touch people's hearts and spirits, making for a memorable experience. There, friends, families, and theater enthusiasts congregate to see the magic take place on stage. The collective guffaws, gasps, and cheers create a lovely symphony that heightens the festive spirit.

NYC CHRISTMAS

- **Lunt-Fontanne Theatre:**

Known for its diverse range of shows, it features enchanting performances that resonate with the festive season. The Lunt-Fontanne Theatre is a prestigious venue located at 205 West 46th Street in the thriving Theater District. Its position entices theatergoers and holiday revelers to experience Broadway's magic during this festive season. The Lunt-Fontanne Theatre's distinctive marquee draws attention and teases you with the exciting acts taking place inside.

As soon as you walk through the doors, the stories of the season come to life and fill the room with enthusiasm. The Lunt-Fontanne Theatre's holiday ambience is mesmerizing. The visually stunning interiors serve as the backdrop for the enthralling performances. You are taken to a magical and wonder-filled world by the performances, which have been specially chosen for the season.

NYC CHRISTMAS

- **Broadhurst Theatre:**

A venue with a unique charm, showcasing special holiday shows that captivate both locals and visitors, making the season brighter. The Broadhurst Theatre has a fantastic location at 235 West 44th Street in the center of the Theater District. It draws both theater connoisseurs and those seeking the romance of Broadway during the Christmas celebrations.

You can't help but be attracted by its elegant marquee, a familiar sight in the middle of Times Square's flashing lights. Stepping inside the theater, you're greeted into a warm atmosphere, where the performances take you to another planet, engaging your senses. The Broadhurst Theatre has a warm, welcoming atmosphere over the holiday season. The charming performances were placed in the interiors, which had a hint of old elegance. The performances, which were specially chosen for the time of year, inspire awe and nostalgia.

NYC CHRISTMAS

❖ **The New York Botanical Garden:**

Offers stunning outdoor light displays and seasonal performances, creating a magical Christmas experience. This vast garden, found in the Bronx at 2900 Southern Boulevard, adds a touch of the outdoors to the urban environment. Its convenient location welcomes both nature lovers and anyone looking to experience the beauty of Christmas among greenery.

It gives this soothing display of lights and holiday decorations. The magnificence that awaits within is already foreshadowed by the entryway. You are thrust into a realm where nature and lights coexist together. The New York Botanical Garden has an exquisite ambience throughout the holiday season. You are led through a winter wonderland by the warmly illuminated walkways. It is a lovely stroll since the trees and plants are decorated with glistening lights, creating a spellbinding sight. People from all walks of life congregate at The New

NYC CHRISTMAS

York Botanical Garden to see how nature's beauty is woven into the holiday celebration of Christmas. A lovely symphony is created by the mingling of laughter, the delicate rustling of the leaves, and the seasonal tunes. Christmastime at The New York Botanical Garden is an opportunity to fully appreciate the marvels of nature, which will fill your heart with the wonder of the Christmas season.

❖ **The Jazz at Lincoln Center:**

This musical center, located at 10 Columbus Circle, charms the city with its creative appeal. Its Central Park-viewing position makes it a popular meeting place for anyone wishing to experience the beauty of live jazz during the holiday celebrations. You are lured to The Jazz at Lincoln Center's contemporary architecture because it is a symbol of the harmonious fusion of music and culture. The atmosphere is filled with music that captures the genuine spirit of the season. The artistically designed rooms provide the backdrop for exciting

NYC CHRISTMAS

performances. The joyous and passionate musical notes strike a chord in people's emotions and provide an unforgettable aural experience. Young and elderly enthusiasts congregate there to honor the art of jazz and the pleasure of the Christmas season. The cadence of the performances and the collective applause create a symphony that heightens the joyous mood.

❖ **The Nutcracker at various venues:**

Many theaters across the city perform the classic Nutcracker ballet during the holiday season, a true festive tradition. Listed down are venues where you can experience "The Nutcracker" during Christmas:

- **David H. Koch Theater:**

The Nutcracker Event at the David H. Koch Theater in New York City is a holiday ballet extravaganza. David H. Koch Theater, a symbol of culture and art, is located in the center of Lincoln Center. Christmastime sees this famous theater come to life

NYC CHRISTMAS

as it embraces the pleasure of the season with spellbinding renditions of "The Nutcracker." This theater, situated at 20 Lincoln Center Plaza, is an important part of the community's cultural fabric. Everyone is welcome to enjoy the wonder of ballet throughout the Christmas celebrations because of its placement inside the thriving Lincoln Center. The design, which combines beauty and modernism, creates the ideal backdrop for the timeless story of "The Nutcracker." As you enter the theater, you step into a realm where exquisite ballet dancers narrate a tale that has mesmerized centuries.

During the Nutcracker performance, the atmosphere at the David H. Koch Theater becomes magical. The dancers' amazing motions bring the story to life, and the stage is decorated with gorgeous scenery. As Clara travels through the Land of Sweets, the audience joins her on a fantastical adventure. Groups of friends, families, and ballet fans create an atmosphere of shared astonishment and wonder. The children's cheers, squeals of

NYC CHRISTMAS

excitement, and sparkly eyes create a lovely symphony that heightens the festive mood. Attending the Nutcracker performance at the David H. Koch Theater is an opportunity to immerse yourself in the brilliance of ballet. It's an opportunity to take in the beauty of this timeless story, which will leave you feeling the wonder of a live performance and the genuine spirit of the Christmas season.

- **Kings Theatre:**

Nestled in the heart of Brooklyn is the King's Theatre, an architectural marvel that comes alive during Christmas. This iconic theater presents a mesmerizing performance of the timeless story of "The Nutcracker." The Kings Theatre, located at 1027 Flatbush Avenue, is a well-known center of culture in Brooklyn. Everyone is welcome to enjoy the magic of ballet during the holiday celebrations thanks to its historical setting. Its opulent façade immediately grabs your attention. The architecture is a perfect combination of elegance and grandeur, providing the ideal backdrop for the classic story of "The Nutcracker." Stepping inside transports you to a realm where elegant ballet dancers tell a tale that has charmed audiences for decades. The dancers bring the story to life with their elegant movements, and the stage is decorated with stunning scenery.

- **Brooklyn Academy of Music (BAM):**

The famous Brooklyn Academy of Music (BAM) is a cultural sanctuary that glows brightly throughout the holiday season. This facility produces exciting productions of "The Nutcracker," among other unique events. BAM is a Brooklyn institution for creative expression, and its address is 30 Lafayette Avenue. Due to its ideal location inside the borough, everyone is welcome to enjoy the wonder of dance and theater throughout the holiday celebrations. Its distinctive building, a fusion of modernism and heritage, welcomes you. The structure itself is a canvas for imagination, creating the atmosphere for the famous narrative of "The Nutcracker." When you go inside, you enter a world

NYC CHRISTMAS

where the arts come to life and tell tales that have captured audiences' attention for decades. Christmastime at BAM is a very festive time there. The anticipation in the theater is palpable as the performers take the stage to bring "The Nutcracker" to life. The audience is taken to a magical world of surprise and joy by the expertly crafted scenery and the dancers' elegant movements.

These locations provide a wonderful array of entertainment options, showcasing the festive spirit and adding to the joy of Christmas in New York City.

NYC CHRISTMAS

CREATING YOUR CHRISTMAS ITINERARY

One-Day Christmas Blitz: Make Every Moment Count

Arriving in New York during the holidays? With this one-day Christmas schedule, you can fully experience the enchantment of the season while making every moment special. Take advantage of the holiday cheer, sparkle, and fun that this lovely city provides.

Morning:

- First, Start your day at this venerable center of festive happiness, the Rockefeller Center. Admire the majestic Christmas tree and delight in the charming ice rink. The merry accents will make your day seem just like Christmas.

NYC CHRISTMAS

- St. Patrick's Cathedral architectural marvel is close by and well worth a visit. The Christmas decorations complement the Cathedral's breathtaking grandeur, giving it a peaceful beginning to your day.

Midday:

- Visit well-known seasonal Holiday Markets including Union Square seasonal Market and Bryant Park Winter Village. Enjoy the festive booths, discover one-of-a-kind presents, and indulge in mouthwatering holiday delights.

- Grab a snack at one of the markets' many seasonal food kiosks. Enjoy traditional Christmas treats while taking in the festive ambiance.

NYC CHRISTMAS

Noon:

- Exercise off your lunch at Central Park. Take in the breathtaking winter scenery and possibly ride in a horse-drawn carriage for a traditional Christmas experience.

- To see the renowned Christmas window decorations at shops like Macy's, Saks Fifth Avenue, and others, take a trip along Fifth Avenue. Every window offers a beautiful view.

Evening:

- Take in a Christmas-themed production to really experience Broadway's charm. The theaters are decked up in festive splendor, which gives the show an added touch of magic.

NYC CHRISTMAS

- Choose a restaurant with a festive atmosphere. Enjoy a delicious supper while taking in the festive ambiance.

Night:

- Visit Dyker Heights in Brooklyn to round off your day, where houses are decked up in lavish Christmas decorations. It's a real show and the ideal way to wrap out your Christmas blitz.

By following this schedule, you can and will make the most of your day and fully experience the wonder and beauty of Christmas in New York City. Enjoy every second and make treasured memories.

NYC CHRISTMAS

Holiday Getaway for Two Days: Double the Joy

Utilize this lovely two-day festive plan to soak in New York's jovial holiday vibe. As you visit the city's well-known Christmas sights, let the romance of the occasion engulf you.

Day 1. Morning:

- Start your day off with a stroll in Central Park. Enjoy the brisk winter air and the festive charm that this renowned park emits over the holiday season.

- Pick a quaint café nearby and have a substantial breakfast while basking in the warmth of a delicious meal.

- Visit MoMA (Museum of Modern Art) to feel the ingenuity and artistic expression of people. Your cultural tour has a festive feel thanks to the museum's holiday decorations.

- Visit the Tour of Radio City Music Hall storied location with a guided tour. Discover its history while potentially catching sight of the renowned Rockettes practicing for the Christmas performances.

Afternoon:

- Enjoy a great meal in a cafe that reflects the Christmas mood while indulging in delectable food in a welcoming setting.

- To experience the festive enchantment of the city, board a tour bus. You will be mesmerized by the city's merry decorations and vivacious atmosphere.

NYC CHRISTMAS

Evening:

- Enjoy a traditional New York City restaurant for supper. The lively atmosphere and exquisite dishes will enhance your evening.

- A Broadway show is a great way to round off your first day. You will be completely engrossed in the enchantment of live entertainment by the show's energy and brilliance.

Day 2. Morning:

- Take a refreshing stroll along The High Line, an elevated park with beautiful vistas, to start your day. The wintery allure gives it a unique attraction.

- Enjoy breakfast at a hip café nearby to fully immerse yourself in the modern feel of the city.

NYC CHRISTMAS

- Explore the crowded streets of the city and take in the lavish Christmas window displays at numerous big retailers.

- Visit the Empire State Building to take in the city's mesmerizing panoramic vistas.

Afternoon:

- Enjoy lunch at a holiday market, where the festive atmosphere and seasonal treats are plentiful.

- Take pleasure in the sport of ice skating in Bryant Park while taking in the lively ambiance of Bryant Park's Winter Village.

Evening:

- Explore the lovely Grand Central Terminal, which has been exquisitely decorated for the

NYC CHRISTMAS

occasion. The Christmas spirit is amplified by the architecture and activity.

- Pick a restaurant with a festive atmosphere. Enjoy a delicious supper while taking in the festive atmosphere.

Night:

- To round off your merry vacation, take a night bus trip to take in the city's glistening lights and decorations.

This two-day schedule ensures that you experience twice as much holiday happiness while celebrating Christmas in the heart of New York City and making lifelong memories.

NYC CHRISTMAS

Fun Christmas Activities for the Whole Family

Embrace the excitement of the festive season in New York City with this Christmas schedule that is suitable for families. This excursion delivers priceless experiences for everyone and is designed to please all ages.

Day 1. Morning:

- Enjoy a delicious breakfast to start the day in a vintage New York cafe. The relaxed ambiance is the ideal setting for a day of family time.

- Go to Central Park, a lush haven right in the middle of the city. The parents can take a leisurely walk around the festive surroundings while the kids run about and play.

NYC CHRISTMAS

- Take the kids to a family-friendly museum like the Children's Museum of Manhattan, where the young ones will be engaged and thrilled by the interactive displays.

- Enjoy a family meal at a place renowned for its inviting atmosphere and kid-friendly food.

Afternoon:

- Take part in a session where the entire family can make Christmas ornaments or decorations;

Christmas crafting events are available in several locations over the holiday season, allowing you to express your creativity while creating fun holiday-themed projects with loved ones. In New York, you have the following alternatives for holiday crafting:

NYC CHRISTMAS

- **The Craft Studio:** The Craft Studio, which is in Manhattan, provides a variety of Christmas crafts classes. They provide a festive creating experience for all ages, one will experience ornament decorating as well as DIY Christmas crafts.

- **Brooklyn Craft Company:** This Brooklyn-based creative community often offers unique holiday-making courses. You will discover a selection of imaginative Christmas-themed programs, crafts like creating customized holiday cards and building decorations.

- **Michaels:** Michaels is a well-known arts and crafts retailer with several locations around New York City. Michaels sometimes hosts holiday crafting events and courses. For Christmastime scheduling and availability, check their website or go to a local shop.

NYC CHRISTMAS

- **Jo-Ann Craft and Fabric Store:** Another well-known craft retailer is Jo-Ann, which has many locations in New York City. They host Christmas crafting events where you can learn how to make festive crafts and decorations.

- **The New York Public Library (NYPL):** Holiday crafting events are sometimes held by the NYPL, particularly at the locations with maker spaces. During the holiday season, check the library's events schedule for craft sessions appropriate for different age groups.

- **CraftJam:** CraftJam provides crafting classes at various sites across NYC. They offer special sessions throughout the holiday season where students will learn how to make wreaths, decorations, and other festive crafts.

NYC CHRISTMAS

These locations provide chances to participate in the festive making fun and make lovely Christmas-themed decorations and presents. To guarantee you get a seat for Christmas crafts, check out their websites for timetables and reservations.

- Whenever a joyful holiday-themed train is available, ride it. The youngsters will be enthralled by the festive atmosphere and decorations on board.

Everyone enjoys the delight of taking a holiday train during the Christmas season in New York. Below are locations where you can board a cheery train and take in the Christmas spirit:

- **The Polar Express exhibit at the New York Historical Society:** Families can take the wonderful Polar Express train trip while donning comfy pajamas, sipping hot chocolate, and listening to the timeless tale.

NYC CHRISTMAS

It's a fun journey that both children and adults will enjoy.

- **Holiday Train Show at the New York Transit Museum:** The Brooklyn-based Transit Museum presents a charming holiday train show each year. Visitors are mesmerized by the dazzling display of New York sites as miniature trains pass past it.

- **New York Botanical Garden Holiday Train performance:** At the New York Botanical Garden, you will see a spectacular train performance that has model trains zipping through a scale-model version of New York City that is decked up for the holidays.

As you travel through small landscapes and take pleasure in the holiday atmosphere on these lovely train trips, these Christmas train experiences in New York bring the magic of Christmas to life. It's a

NYC CHRISTMAS

lovely way to enjoy the holiday season with loved ones.

Evening:

- Indulge in supper in a restaurant decked out in holiday décor as you embrace the joyous spirit of the season.

- Take a tour of the city's stunning Christmas lights by bus or trolley. The glistening lights and colorful decorations will mesmerize the small ones.

Day 2.Morning:

- Bring the family to Santa's Workshop, a location where Santa resides so that the kids may tell him about their Christmas desires.

NYC CHRISTMAS

- Enjoy a themed breakfast with characters or holiday delicacies to add a little enchantment to your morning.

- Watch a Christmas movie with the family at a park or local theater while enjoying popcorn and soft blankets.

- Take the family to a crowded food market for lunch to experience a festive ambiance.

Afternoon:

- Take the family to a nearby ice rink where they can all have fun ice skating, a traditional Christmas pastime.

- Take the kids to a classic candy store where they can savor delicious holiday sweets. It's fun to visit candy stores in New York around Christmas. They resemble candy-filled fantasy worlds where you will discover a

NYC CHRISTMAS

variety of seasonal delicacies. They're packed with sweet treats, like holiday chocolates and candy canes. They are seen around Central Park as well as in busy districts like Times Square, Rockefeller Center, and others.

Evening:

- Select a restaurant with a vibrant atmosphere and a unique holiday menu to make it a memorable family meal.

- Finish the day by singing Christmas carols to others in your neighborhood or at a nearby event to share holiday cheer.

Everyone will have a wonderful journey while creating priceless memories on this family-friendly Christmas itinerary. Together, enjoy the wonder and delight of the festive season.

NYC CHRISTMAS

Romantic Christmas Escape: Love in the air

Set off on a merry Christmas adventure in New York while celebrating love and the jolly holiday spirit. This itinerary guarantees a romantic getaway that will help you and your partner make priceless memories.

Day 1. Morning:

- Set the tone for a warm and private day by starting your day with a delicious breakfast at a Bistro.

- Walk hand in hand across Central Park and take in its tranquil beauty as it is decorated for the winter.

- Visit a nearby gallery of art to admire the inventiveness and possibly discover a work that speaks to your romantic history. Explore

NYC CHRISTMAS

these vivid art spaces that come to life in New York during the joyous Christmas season:

→ **Metropolitan Museum of Art" (Met):** Situated at 1000 Fifth Avenue, the Met offers a cultural Christmas experience by showcasing a variety of art collections.

→ **The Museum of Modern Art (MoMA):** MoMA, which is located at 11 West 53rd Street, features modern and contemporary art while celebrating creativity throughout the holidays.

→ **Guggenheim Museum:** Located at 1071 Fifth Avenue, the Guggenheim has avant-garde art displays, giving your Christmas art study a distinctive flair.

→ **The Whitney Museum of American Art:** The Whitney Museum, which displays

NYC CHRISTMAS

American modern art and welcomes holiday fans, is tucked away at 99 Gansevoort Street.

→ **The Met Cloisters:** The Met Cloisters, located at 99 Margaret Corbin Drive, showcases medieval European art and takes visitors on a historical tour throughout the holiday season.

→ **The Frick Collection:** The Frick Collection, located at 1 East 70th Street, is home to a spectacular collection of European artwork and offers a relaxing vacation art experience.

→ **American Museum of Natural History:** Located at 200 Central Park West, the American Museum of Natural History mixes art with the marvels of the natural world and is a wonderful place to visit over the holiday season.

NYC CHRISTMAS

- Share a peaceful lunch at a quaint café while enjoying delectable food in a welcoming and romantic setting.

Afternoon:

- Feel the intimacy and romanticism in the wintertime air as you travel in a horse-drawn carriage around Central Park.

- Visit Top of the Rock at Rockefeller Center for sweeping city vistas that will strengthen your relationship with the recognizable New York City skyline.

Evening:

- Take advantage of a fine dining establishment's beautiful meal to enhance your romantic Christmas getaway.

NYC CHRISTMAS

- End the evening with a Broadway performance to immerse yourself in the realm of live entertainment and creative genius.

Day 2.Morning:

- Take a breathtaking helicopter ride above New York City to take in the city's spectacular magnificence.

- Enjoy a romantic breakfast with your significant other while taking in the breathtaking views from a rooftop restaurant.

- Choose meaningful presents for one another as a way to show your affection for one another by going Christmas shopping together.

NYC CHRISTMAS

- Enjoy the Christmas spirit and the delight of being together as you glide hand in hand over the ice at a lovely skating rink.

- Explore The Met Cloisters, a magical museum, and let the antiquated artwork and architecture carry you away to an era of classic romance.

- Visit a neighboring vineyard for a great wine-tasting experience and a romantic location to celebrate your relationship. Explore the bustling wineries that invite tourists to New York during the joyous Christmas season:

→ **Brooklyn Winery:** Located at 213 N 8th Street, Brooklyn Winery extends a cordial invitation to wine lovers and offers tastings as well as a friendly environment throughout the festive season.

NYC CHRISTMAS

→ **City Winery:** Located at 25 11th Avenue, City Winery welcomes you to partake in wonderful wines while celebrating the season and experiencing the pleasure of winemaking.

→ **The Red Hook Winery:** Red Hook Winery, located at 175-204 Van Dyke Street, offers a magnificent setting to enjoy wines and take part in seasonal events.

→ **Rooftop Reds:** Situated at 299 Sands Street, Rooftop Reds provides a unique vineyard experience that lets you sip wine and take in the holiday splendor of the city.

→ **Brotherhood, the oldest winery in the United States:** Brotherhood Winery is a historic place located at 100 Brotherhood Plaza Drive where you will enjoy wines in a festive atmosphere.

NYC CHRISTMAS

Evening:

- Sail on the glistening waters while enjoying a romantic evening cruise with city lights as a background.

- Finish your romantic break with a calm and private evening at your preferred lodging, cherishing the memories made throughout your magical Christmas vacation.

With love in the air and a spectacular Christmas experience for you and your companion, this romantic Christmas itinerary in New York guarantees a lovely retreat. May the warmth of the season and the pleasure of the season fill your hearts.

NYC CHRISTMAS

NYC Christmas on a Budget: Have Fun Without Breaking the Bank

Without breaking the bank, enjoy the wonder of Christmas in New York City. This schedule is designed for those who wish to take full advantage of the holiday season without breaking the bank.

Day 1. Morning:

- Start your day in a nearby café with reasonably priced coffee and breakfast from the bakery to give you energy for the day.

- Take a cheap morning walk across Central Park to see the park's natural splendor and capture the spirit of the season.

- Go to the Christmas markets, including those in Union Square and Columbus Circle, to take in the cheer and maybe locate some inexpensive presents.

NYC CHRISTMAS

- Lunch can be had for a reasonable price at one of the numerous food trucks or kiosks located around the city.

Afternoon:

- Visit institutions that allow free or pay-what-you-wish admission, such as the American Museum of Natural History or the Museum at the Fashion Institute of Technology.

- Visit Bryant Park's Winter Village for the day, taking in the decorations and possibly participating in some reasonably priced holiday activities.

Evening:

- Enjoy a filling supper at a vintage NYC restaurant that is renowned for its inexpensive but tasty fare.

NYC CHRISTMAS

- A cheap option to get into the Christmas mood is to end the day with a self-guided tour of the city's holiday lights.

Day 2.Morning:

- Having breakfast at a neighborhood bagel store is a classic New York experience.

- Obtain stunning views of the Statue of Liberty and the Manhattan skyline by taking a free trip on the Staten Island Ferry.

- Take a stroll around Chinatown neighborhood, where you can have lunch that is both inexpensive and authentically Chinese.

- Take a stroll along Fifth Avenue while viewing the lavish Christmas window decorations.

NYC CHRISTMAS

Afternoon:

- Explore famous libraries, like the New York Public Library, which provides free access and a calm reading area.

- Look for free workshops or demos taking place across the city, sometimes with a Christmas theme.

Evening:

- Enjoy supper at a food truck, where you will discover a choice of reasonably priced and delectable selections.

- Attend a public tree-lighting ceremony in the city. These events are often free to the public and filled with holiday happiness.

This inexpensive Christmas schedule makes sure that you have a wonderful holiday in New York

NYC CHRISTMAS

City without breaking the bank. Embrace the holiday cheer while being mindful of your spending and making enduring Christmas memories in the city.

NYC CHRISTMAS

EXPLORING CHRISTMAS DELIGHTS IN NYC

A Visual Feast of the Best Neighborhoods for Holiday Decorations

New York City's streets are transformed into a captivating sight of seasonal happiness when the holiday season arrives. These areas provide a feast for the eyes when it comes to Christmas decorations:

- **Dyker Heights in Brooklyn:**

Brooklyn's Dyker Heights is transformed into a glittering paradise throughout the holiday season. The southwestern Brooklyn neighborhood decorates its houses for the holidays with elaborate and lavish decorations. Every home strives to make the most eye-catching arrangement of lights, figurines, and holiday decorations. As people pass past, awestruck by the imagination and work put into these magnificent displays, the streets come alive with the

NYC CHRISTMAS

joyful atmosphere of the season. It's a wonderful event that captures the actual spirit of Christmas and makes people feel in amazement and joy.

- **Upper West Side:**

The Upper West Side, located in the western portion of Manhattan, dons a captivating festive cloak throughout the holiday season. The lovely stores and quaint brownstones are festooned with a variety of holiday accents. Warm light is projected on the busy walkways as sparkling lights dance over the streets. Walking through these streets is a lovely experience because of the festive atmosphere created by the decorated trees and wreaths. This neighborhood's realistic depiction of the Christmas' spirit makes everyone who visits happy and gives them a feeling of community.

- **Gramercy Park:**

Gramercy Park, located in the center of Manhattan, is transformed into a winter paradise throughout the holiday season. The area, which is renowned for its

NYC CHRISTMAS

ancient attractiveness, has a mystical aspect. Wreaths and festive lights on brownstones convey a feeling of age-old joy. You can't help but be enthralled by the warm atmosphere and the festive spirit as you stroll through the snow-covered streets. It is a location where the Christmas spirit comes to life, engulfing you in the happiness and splendor of the season.

- **Park Slope, Brooklyn:**

Park Slope is a neighborhood in southern Brooklyn that transforms into a dazzling festive wonderland during the Christmas season. The streets are decorated with snowflakes, and residences are alive with a variety of holiday accents. Each home participates in a friendly competition to display the most lights and decorations, turning the neighborhood into a beautiful winter paradise. Families and groups of friends stroll through the picturesque streets while beaming from ear to ear at the lovely decorations. In Park Slope, the holiday

NYC CHRISTMAS

cheer is shared with everyone who passes through the neighborhood's brightly lit streets.

- **Bay Ridge, Brooklyn:**

Southwest of the borough in Brooklyn lies Bay Ridge, which transforms into a magnificent display throughout the holiday season. Homes in the area are decked up in a kaleidoscope of vibrant lights and ornaments, embracing the holiday mood. Through their decorations, each home offers its own Christmas story that wins the hearts of onlookers. As families assemble to see this group effort to spread happiness, the streets are filled with the festive spirit of the season. Bay Ridge is the epitome of the holiday spirit, illuminating the neighborhood with cheer and warmth and demonstrating the harmony and happiness of the neighborhood.

Queens:

Christmastime sees Queens, a multicultural borough in New York City, turn into a holiday haven.

NYC CHRISTMAS

Neighborhoods from Astoria to Forest Hills come to life with the sparkle of holiday lights and ornaments. The neighborhood is filled with Christmas cheer, and each house proudly displays its festive attitude. In this collective celebration, families and friends come together, beaming as they walk through the festive streets. Queens is a wonderful location to experience the enchantment of the season since it embodies the lovely tapestry of cultures and customs and melds them into a seamless Christmas celebration.

- **Washington Square Park Area:**

The vicinity of Washington Square Park, which is in the center of Greenwich Village, is a delightful haven during the holiday season. The park is illuminated by tall trees decked up with sparkling lights, which creates a cozy and festive atmosphere. Street musicians' jubilant tunes are carried into the air, adding to the celebration. The colorful street sellers selling a variety of seasonal goodies grab the attention of onlookers. In this energetic and bustling

NYC CHRISTMAS

area of New York City, families assemble to take in the festive mood and capture the true spirit of Christmas.

- **SoHo:**

SoHo emits a stylish holiday vibe, with stores and creative installations adding to the area's upscale and up-to-date festive ambiance.

When you explore these areas during the Christmas season, you'll be treated to a visual feast as you take in the breathtaking variety of decorations that characterize the beauty of Christmas in New York City. Your Christmas season will be memorable because of the distinct and wonderful experiences offered by each community.

NYC CHRISTMAS

Delicious Christmas food and treats: Experience the Season

The gastronomic experience of Christmas in New York will have your taste senses dancing with joy. The city's cafes and bakeries embrace the Christmas season with a lovely selection of festive delicacies. Imagine yourself being tempted to experience the actual flavor of winter by the warm, fragrant, roasted chestnuts being served on street corners. The tempting aroma of steaming hot chocolate tempts you to wrap your hands around a cup that is topped with a swirl of creamy marshmallows.

Restaurants in the city's center decorate their menus with holiday specialties as they enjoy the pleasure of the season. Family-friendly restaurants provide roast turkey, glazed ham, and all the fixings, encouraging you to enjoy a hearty lunch with loved ones. Wandering around the varied districts will allow you to sample a variety of delicacies from across the world that have been given a festive

NYC CHRISTMAS

touch. A wonderful symphony of herbs and spices reflects the city's diverse fabric. Remember to enjoy the delicious treats that Christmas provides! Yule logs, gingerbread biscuits, and fruitcakes are displayed in bakeries in enticing arrays; each mouthful evokes nostalgia and tradition. The aroma of recently made pies and sweets permeates the air, encouraging you to indulge in the festive spirit.

New York City's culinary landscape welcomes you to savor the holidays, be it that you decide to choose a cozy bakery in Brooklyn, a busy diner in Midtown, or a family-run restaurant in Queens. Christmas in the Big Apple is defined by the tantalizing fragrances, warm atmosphere, and delectable delights that come together to make the occasion.

NYC CHRISTMAS

Top NYC Restaurant Picks for a Cozy Christmas Meal: Warming Restaurants

❖ Tavern on the Green:

The lovely atmosphere of Tavern on the Green, a hidden treasure located in 67th Street & Central Park West, draws people in. During the holiday season, this famous restaurant, which is surrounded by the park's natural splendor, transforms into a warm refuge. The pleasant warmth that awaits within is hinted at by the exterior's glittering lighting. Once inside, the atmosphere enchants; the simple but stylish design whisks you away to a winter wonderland. The sound of joyful discussions combines with the crackling of the fireplace to create a cozy atmosphere. Christmas dining at this restaurant is like taking part in a touching story, where delectable cuisine and the spirit of the season combine to produce an amazing experience.

NYC CHRISTMAS

❖ Serendipity 3:

Serendipity 3 is a paradise for fans of Christmas, conveniently located on Manhattan's busy Upper East Side precisely on; 225 E 60th St. This famous restaurant comes to life with a whimsical appeal as the festive season fills the city with cheer. You are taken to a winter wonderland by the intimate restaurant's décor, which is decked up in holiday decorations and dazzling lights.

The air is filled with the aroma of freshly baked goods, and a cheery atmosphere is produced by chatting and laughing. The menu has delicious beverages and sweets with festive themes that beckon you to indulge in the season's sweet mood. Serendipity 3 is a must-experience stop for anybody looking to experience the genuine pleasure of Christmas in New York City at this time of year since a visit during this period conjures the sheer enchantment of the season.

NYC CHRISTMAS

❖ **The Bryant Park Grill:**

The Bryant Park Grill, a refuge of warmth and gastronomic pleasure during the Christmas season, is located among the dazzling lights and festive fun of Bryant Park's Winter Village. This welcoming restaurant, located in Midtown Manhattan, (25 W 40th St.) Provides the ideal combination of gourmet food and festive pleasure. Visitors are enticed inside by the exterior's inviting, rustic appeal, which transports them to a world decorated for Christmas. As soon as you enter, you are embraced by the atmosphere, which is a calming fusion of tasteful design and jovial conversation. A memorable dining experience that captures the genuine spirit of the festive season is made possible by the setting and the delicious meal.

❖ **Bubby's High Line:**

In the bustling Chelsea area, next to the charming High Line park (120 Hudson St,) Bubby's High Line transforms into a warm refuge during the holiday season. Bubby's does not hide its festive

NYC CHRISTMAS

cheer as the neighborhood does. You are greeted with a cozy light as you enter the restaurant. A taste of Christmas is promised by the aroma of warming, substantial dinners filling the air. As guests assemble to partake in a substantial lunch and celebrate the pleasure of the season, laughter and conversation fill the quaint nooks. A wonderful getaway, Bubby's High Line invites you to enjoy the Christmas delicacies among the splendor of the city.

❖ **Brooklyn Farmacy & Soda Fountain:**

The Brooklyn Farmacy & Soda Fountain, located in Carroll Gardens, Brooklyn (513 Henry St,) evokes holiday nostalgia throughout the holiday season. Entering is like traveling through time, as the festive spirit is celebrated with a retro flair. Festive accents are added to the warm atmosphere, creating a welcoming environment. The aroma of mouthwatering food and the sound of pleasant conversations fill the air. Families and friends go here to savor the festive fare that makes them think of a bygone Christmas. In the coziest of settings, it offers a taste of the holidays by fusing the past with the present.

❖ **Gramercy Tavern:**

In the heart of Manhattan's bustling streets (42 E 20th St). Gramercy Tavern shines brightly with winter happiness throughout the Christmas season. This quaint eatery in the Gramercy area offers a kind welcome to guests in the spirit of the time of year. As soon as you enter, the sophisticated but welcoming interior will take you to a winter wonderland.

There is a festive expectation in the air due to the warm glow of the lights and the delicious aroma of the holiday food. The holiday meals are thoughtfully designed and aim to take diners on a delicious culinary tour of tastes and customs. You are invited to enjoy Christmas at Gramercy Tavern where the holiday spirit permeates every nook and cranny.

NYC CHRISTMAS

❖ **Café Lalo:**

Café Lalo on Manhattan's Upper West Side comes alive with festive cheer throughout the Christmas season. This charming café, which is located on a busy street (201 W 83rd St), attracts residents and tourists looking for a little holiday cheer. With the romantic glow of the lights and the soothing scent of freshly made coffee, the atmosphere is lovely. Wall and window decorations evoke the festive spirit of the season. The lovely selection of food and hot drinks on the menu beckons you to relax and take in the festivities. The bustling streets of New York City are the ideal setting for the warm-hearted spirit of Christmas, and Café Lalo offers just that.

These restaurants are the perfect places to have a special Christmas meal in the heart of New York City because they combine delicious cuisine with a cozy ambiance.

NYC CHRISTMAS

Family-Friendly Christmas Dining in NYC: A Warm Welcome

Christmas in New York City is magical, and family-friendly restaurants. They will take you to the ideal fusion of celebration and pleasure. Enter a world of warmth and delight with your loved ones in tow.

❖ **Ellen's Stardust Diner**

Ellen's Stardust Diner, located in the center of Times Square (1650 Broadway), shines with happiness throughout the holiday season. The restaurant, which is just a short distance from the colorful Broadway lights, transforms into a jovial hive of holiday pleasure. The recognizable vintage sign invites you to a world of music and fun as you get closer. The buzz of talks and family laughing fills the room, creating an electrifying environment. The brilliant waitstaff enters the stage with contagious zeal and serenades the crowd with well-known songs. The furnishings have a retro

NYC CHRISTMAS

appeal that transports you to the height of enjoyment. Ellen's Stardust Diner is a must-go location to experience the enchantment of Christmas in the middle of the city since it perfectly captures the spirit of the season.

❖ Patsy's Italian Restaurant

Located in the center of Midtown Manhattan (236 W 56th St), Patsy's Italian Restaurant extends a warm greeting to visitors over the holiday season. A short distance from Times Square's bustle, this family-friendly restaurant has a classic charm. The small environment is ideal for a Christmas gathering thanks to the red-checkered tablecloths and subtle lighting. All who arrive are enticed by the air's seductive scent of Italian food. Families gather around tables to tell tales and enjoy authentic Italian cuisine. The atmosphere and food at Patsy's Italian Restaurant are reminiscent of the coziness and camaraderie of the Christmas season.

NYC CHRISTMAS

❖ The Mermaid Inn

The Mermaid Inn in New York City's 570 Amsterdam Ave, transforms into a paradise of seashore pleasures throughout the holiday season. This lively neighborhood restaurant, which is welcoming to families, captures the mood of the seashore in the middle of the city. A happy eating experience is ensured by the nautical theme that adorns the inviting environment. Families assemble to savor the aromas of the sea, creating an atmosphere reminiscent of a coastal vacation. A mouthwatering variety of seafood is included on the menu, exciting the senses and providing a taste of the holidays in a marine environment.

❖ Cowgirl

Cowgirl, tucked away in Lower Manhattan (519 Hudson St and 259 Front Street), is a charming place to spend Christmas. This family-friendly restaurant, tucked away in a bustling area, whisks you away to a welcoming seaside getaway. As you get closer, your eye is drawn to the colorful facade decorated with seahorses. The interior is lively and beachy, with bright lights and decorations with nautical themes. Families gather around tables to enjoy mouthwatering food with Southern and Mexican influences. The sound of clients laughing fills the air and reflects the festive mood. A special Christmas eating experience is provided by Cowgirl Seahorse, which combines the joy of the season with a coastal, nautical flair.

❖ **Brooklyn Farmacy & Soda Fountain**

The Brooklyn Farmacy & Soda Fountain, which is located in Carroll Gardens, Brooklyn at 513 Henry St, transforms into a cozy refuge for the holiday season. This family-friendly location is tucked away in an area renowned for its sense of camaraderie, and it exudes timeless charm. The facade, which is festooned with wreaths and dazzling lights, beckons onlookers into a warm past. The interior's retro furnishings revive recollections of a gentler period. Families congregate at the counter while ogling the delicious menu with interest. A cozy festive ambiance is created by the scent of delicious food and the buzz of laughing. Brooklyn Farmacy & Soda Fountain provides a beautiful taste of Christmas in the middle of Brooklyn while also offering delectable treats and a trip back in time.

❖ **Max Brenner**

Max Brenner, a coffee shop located in Manhattan's Union Square at 841 Broadway, is transformed into a chocolate paradise during the holiday. As you enter, the city's busy streets give way to a cozy and welcoming ambiance. The air is filled with the delicious aroma of chocolate, which immediately causes happiness and anticipation. All guests are charmed by the interior's fascinating blend of a contemporary restaurant and a comfortable chocolate refuge, which has whimsical details. Families gather to enjoy a buffet laden with chocolate while drinking from recognizable Hug Mugs and indulging in decadently sweet treats. Max Brenner transforms into a haven of chocolate treats,

NYC CHRISTMAS

encouraging you to experience the wonder of Christmas in a cocoa-infused environment.

❖ **Junior's Restaurant**

Junior's Restaurant, located in the bustling atmosphere of 1515 Broadway, 45th Street between Broadway & 8th Ave, experiences a beautiful metamorphosis throughout the holiday. It draws both residents and tourists in with its recognizable signs and warm ambiance. The eatery is filled with holiday cheer and is decked up in festive décor. Families assemble around tables, the prospect of a delicious supper lighting up their cheeks. A hearty and cozy eating experience is promised by the air's intoxicating scent of traditional American meals.

Each of these restaurants offers a unique dining experience perfect for families during the Christmas season.

NYC CHRISTMAS

ACCOMMODATIONS

Christmas Retreats: Luxurious Accommodations in the Heart of NYC

A selection of places to stay in New York for a memorable Christmas is provided below:

❖ **The Plaza Hotel**
The Plaza Hotel, which towers above Central Park's southeast corner at 768 Fifth Avenue, is a symbol of opulence and is particularly charming during the holiday. It is a beautiful sight when it is decorated for the holidays. Visitors are welcomed into an elegant environment at the entryway, which is decorated with wreaths and garlands. The foyer establishes a regal tone with its lofty ceilings and traditional furniture. Families congregate in the comfortable sitting areas as excitement fills the room. The hallways lead to chambers that combine contemporary comfort with classic splendor. The Plaza Hotel's great position affords visitors a view

NYC CHRISTMAS

of Central Park and an invitation to take in the holiday spirit in classic New York fashion.

❖ The Ritz-Carlton

The Ritz-Carlton Hotel in New York, which is elegantly situated on 50 Central Park South, transforms into a beacon of luxury and holiday elegance. It's a wonderful sight, all decked up in stylish Christmas décor. All are welcomed into a world of sophisticated elegance by the entryway, which is decorated with wreaths and sparkling lights. The foyer has a warm and welcoming ambiance thanks to its opulent chandeliers and comfortable furnishings. Families and visitors assemble, looking forward to the season's delights. The chic and comfortable apartments provide a pleasant haven to take in the magic of Christmas in the middle of the city. The Ritz-Carlton Hotel invites you to celebrate the holidays in traditional New York style thanks to its ideal position, which offers vistas of Central Park.

❖ The Pierre, A Taj Hotel

NYC CHRISTMAS

The Pierre, A Taj Hotel is a wonderful location, particularly during the Christmas season. It is gracefully positioned on 2 East 61st Street at 5th Avenue. The hotel is surrounded by lovely seasonal decorations and exudes a wonderful air. The gateway gives a kind welcome with its festive lighting and wreaths. The elegant and charming foyer welcomes visitors into a world of comfort and luxury. Families and guests congregate, embracing the holiday mood. The rooms, a haven of luxury and leisure, provide a pleasant stay despite the festive commotion. The Pierre, which is located in a superb Fifth Avenue location and invites everyone to experience the pleasure of Christmas in the heart of New York, offers vistas of the bustling metropolis.

❖ The St. Regis

The St. Regis in New York epitomizes class and celebration during the Christmas season as it stands elegantly at the intersection of Two East 55th Street and Fifth Avenue. The hotel is decked up in

NYC CHRISTMAS

stunning Christmas decorations and comes to life with dazzling lights and wreaths, inviting onlookers into an opulent realm. The foyer greets visitors with a touch of opulence and welcomes them with a symphony of elegant design and warmth. Families and visitors congregate, their faces beaming with festive cheer. The rooms, which combine elegance and comfort, provide a quiet haven among the Christmas commotion. The St. Regis encourages everyone to savor the enchantment of Christmas in the center of the city thanks to its great position, which offers a view of Fifth Avenue's busy shopping district.

❖ **The Lotte New York Palace**

The Lotte New York Palace, which stands gracefully at the corner of 50th Street and 455 Madison Avenue, is a wonder during the Christmas season. It is a beautiful sight when decorated for the holidays. The entryway, which is decorated with glistening lights and holiday wreaths, welcomes everyone into a world of elegant luxury. The foyer

NYC CHRISTMAS

embraces visitors with a combination of contemporary elegance and vintage charm. Families and visitors congregate, joyfully enjoying the festive mood of the time of year. In the middle of the hectic celebrations, the rooms, a sanctuary of luxury and elegance, provide a quiet escape. The Lotte New York Palace enables everyone to experience the enchantment of Christmas in the center of the city thanks to its great position, which provides vistas of the famous St. Patrick's Cathedral.

❖ **The Peninsula New York**

The Peninsula New York, located opulently at 700 Fifth Avenue at 55th Street, is transformed into a winter paradise throughout the holidays. It captures the attention of everyone who passes by with its enchanting display of Christmas lights and ornaments. Everyone is welcomed into a world of exquisite luxury and holiday happiness by the entryway, which is decorated with cherry lights and wreaths. The foyer, which exudes warmth and elegance, invites visitors to join in on the festive cheer. Families and guests congregate, celebrating the pleasure and excitement of the season. The rooms, which blend comfort and luxury, provide a quiet haven to take in the holiday commotion. The Peninsula New York welcomes everyone to experience the festive magic in the center of the city thanks to its great position, which provides vistas of Fifth Avenue's busy shopping district.

❖ **The Waldorf Astoria**

The Waldorf Astoria in New York, which graces 301 Park Avenue between 49th and 50th Streets, is a veritable wonder during the holiday season. It has an alluring charm and is decorated with exquisite Christmas decorations. The entryway offers a friendly welcome with its Christmas wreaths and sparkling lighting. The foyer welcomes guests into a realm of elegant luxury and is the picture of timelessness. In the spirit of the holiday season, families and visitors gather together. The luxurious but comfortable rooms give a pleasant haven among

NYC CHRISTMAS

the holiday commotion. The Waldorf Astoria encourages everyone to savor the enchantment of Christmas in the center of the city thanks to its great position that provides vistas of the busy Park Avenue.

❖ **The Carlyle, A Rosewood Hotel**

The Carlyle, A Rosewood Hotel, which is magnificently situated at 35 E 76th Street and Madison Avenue, is transformed into a winter wonderland during the holiday season. It's a beautiful sight when decorated for the holidays. Everyone is welcomed into a world of elegant luxury and holiday happiness at the entryway, which is decorated with dazzling lights and seasonal wreaths. The lobby encourages visitors to enjoy the delight of the festive season with a fusion of warmth and refinement. Together, families and visitors celebrate the holiday spirit. The apartments, which are the height of luxury and comfort, provide a tranquil haven from which to take in the magic of Christmas in the middle of the city. The Carlyle invites everyone to savor the enchantment of Christmas in true New York style thanks to its excellent position, which offers vistas of Madison Avenue.

❖ Mandarin Oriental

The Mandarin Oriental in New York, which is elegantly situated at 80 Columbus Circle, shines with holiday charm throughout the holiday season. The hotel is decorated for the holidays and comes to life with glistening lights and cheery wreaths, enchanting onlookers. Visitors are taken into a world of sophisticated appeal by the entry, an exquisite embrace of warmth and elegance. The joyful anticipation of the season lifts the spirits of families and visitors as they congregate. In the middle of the joyful spirit, the rooms, which mix comfort and modernity, provide a warm haven. The Mandarin Oriental welcomes everyone to take in the enchantment of Christmas in the heart of New York City from its ideal location with views of Central Park and the city skyline.

NYC CHRISTMAS

❖ The Langham

The Langham Hotel in New York, located stylishly at the corner of 400 Fifth Avenue and 36th Street, is a lovely place to visit during the Christmas season. It becomes a spectacular sight when it is decorated with lovely holiday decorations. The entryway spreads a kind and welcoming hug with its decorations of glistening lights and wreaths. The foyer welcomes visitors to the delight of the festive season with its blend of modern elegance and friendly atmosphere.

Families and guests congregate, their hearts brimming with holiday cheer. In the middle of the joyous celebrations, the rooms, a sanctuary of luxury and elegance, provide a tranquil escape. Langham welcomes everyone to take in the magic of Christmas in the heart of the city from its great location next to the famous Empire State Building.

NYC CHRISTMAS

❖ The Beekman, A Thompson Hotel

The Beekman, A Thompson Hotel in New York City, located at the intersection of Beekman and Nassau Streets (123 Nassau Street), turns into a holiday paradise throughout the holiday. It's a sight to see, decked up in alluring Christmas decorations. All are cordially welcomed inside by the entryway, which is festooned with glistening lights and cheery wreaths.

The lobby invites visitors to partake in the festive cheer with its blend of traditional grandeur and cozy atmosphere. Families and guests congregate, savoring the holiday mood. The stylish but comfortable apartments provide a tranquil retreat from the busy celebrations. The Beekman welcomes everyone to experience the wonder of Christmas in the center of the city. It is tucked away in a wonderful position in Lower Manhattan.

NYC CHRISTMAS

❖ The Baccarat Hotel & Residences

The Baccarat Hotel & Residences in New York City, elegantly located on 28 West 53rd Street, is transformed into a wonderful paradise throughout the Christmas season. It exudes a welcoming warmth while being embellished with charming festive accents. All are cordially welcomed into a world of elegant luxury and holiday cheer by the entryway, which is decorated with sparkling lights and seasonal wreaths.

The foyer, which combines comfort and luxury, allows visitors to get into the festive mood. Families and guests congregate, engulfed in the pleasure and fervor of the occasion. The elegantly serene apartments provide a comfortable refuge from the busy celebrations. The Baccarat Hotel & Residences, which is tucked away in the center of Manhattan, invites everyone to take in the magic of Christmas in the busy metropolis.

NYC CHRISTMAS

Budget-Friendly Festive Stays: Cozy Retreats in NYC for Christmas

Here are some pocket-friendly hotels where you can stay comfortably and enjoy the holiday season in New York without spending too much:

❖ **HI NYC Hostel**

The HI NYC Hostel, which is tucked away on 891 Amsterdam Avenue, comes alive with a distinct holiday mood throughout the holiday season. This hostel's lively ambiance embraces the festive spirit, making it a great choice for visitors on a tight budget who want to experience Christmas enthusiasm. Visitors are welcomed by cheery accents and a cozy atmosphere, which promotes a feeling of celebration and community. Due to the hostel's reasonable rates throughout the holiday season, many people choose it to enjoy the romance of Christmas in New York without breaking the bank. During this festive time, rates vary from around $40 to $100 per night, making it an

NYC CHRISTMAS

affordable choice for anyone who wishes to spend the holidays in the city.

❖ Pod 51 Hotel

The Pod 51 Hotel in New York City, which is tucked away on 230 East 51st Street, enjoys a wonderful makeover over the holiday season. The hotel has a welcoming, comfortable ambiance that embraces Christmas pleasure. Due to its central position, visitors can take in the lively celebrations and enjoy the city's holiday decorations. With rates ranging from around $90 to $200 per night for this special occasion, the Pod 51 Hotel provides affordability without sacrificing comfort. This makes it a tempting option for those seeking to get into the festive mood while taking in the busy metropolis without going over budget.

❖ The Jane Hotel:

The Jane Hotel, located on 113 Jane Street, is transformed into a warm refuge during the holiday season. With its festive accents and warm

NYC CHRISTMAS

atmosphere, the hotel exudes a wonderful holiday spirit. Its position puts visitors near the city's holiday commotion, enabling them to take part in the season's joy. The Jane Hotel's rates are from around $100 to $300 per night at this happy time, finding a compromise between cost and comfort. This makes it a desirable option for people looking for a cozy and affordable stay while taking part in the joyful celebrations of Christmas.

❖ **The Local NYC**

The Local NYC hotel, which is located on 13-02 44th Avenue, Long Island City, Queens, is transformed into a warm getaway throughout the holiday season. With exquisite Christmas decorations and a welcoming environment, the hotel exudes a warm and inviting atmosphere.. With rates from around $80 to $250 per night on this particular occasion, The Local NYC provides affordability without sacrificing comfort. This makes it a popular option for tourists looking for a cozy and affordable stay.

NYC CHRISTMAS

❖ Row NYC

The Row NYC hotel, which is located directly on 700 8th Avenue, comes alive with holiday cheer throughout Christmas. The hotel is covered with charming decorations and sparkling lights, bringing the joy of the season within. Guests will immerse themselves in the magical Christmas ambiance that permeates New York thanks to its central downtown location. The Row NYC's reasonable rates, which start from around $120 to $300 per night, provide comfort without breaking the wallet at this happy time. Due to its reasonable price, it attracts travelers looking for a pleasant place to stay while taking part in New York City's holiday celebrations..

❖ The Pod Hotel Times Square

The Pod Hotel in New York City, located close to Times Square precisely; 400 W 42nd St, is transformed into a warm refuge during the holiday season. The hotel is festively decorated for the holidays and exudes a warm welcome. Its excellent location makes it simple for visitors to take in the

NYC CHRISTMAS

vibrant celebrations of Times Square and the nearby Christmas lights. With normal rates that start with $150 up to $300 per night during this particular season, The Pod Hotel provides a mix between comfort and cost. Due to this, it is a well-liked option for tourists seeking to experience the merry atmosphere of Christmas in the city's center without going over their budget.

For visitors seeking to take in the wonder of Christmas in New York City, these lodgings provide a comfortable and affordable respite.

NYC CHRISTMAS

PRACTICAL TRAVEL GUIDE INFORMATION

Dressing Right: Navigating New York's Christmas Weather

Although it might be frigid, New York City has a festive appeal during Christmas. Winters in the city are chilly and brisk, with average lows in December of between 30 and 40 degrees Fahrenheit (-1 to 4 degrees Celsius). Layers are key for comfort, so be sure to include thermal shirts, sweaters, and a high-quality winter coat. To protect yourself from the bitter weather, don't forget to pack a thick hat, gloves, and scarf. As you explore the city, your feet will stay toasty in sturdy, insulated boots. In case of rain or snow, it's also a good idea to carry an umbrella and waterproof shoes. You will enjoy the wonderful holiday season in comfort and elegance if you prepare well for the winter's cold.

NYC CHRISTMAS

Navigating New York's Festive Season: Essential Tips for Travelers

A magnificent experience, visiting New York during Christmas requires planning to ensure a seamless and memorable vacation. First off, reserve lodging well in advance since NYC is quite popular over the holidays. To make the most of your time, plan your schedule and prioritize the sights you want to visit while taking into account their closeness to one another.

Additionally, make use of efficient public transit like buses and subways to save time and money. To stay comfortable in the frigid weather, be sure to wear layers of clothing. The local Christmas specialties, including hot chocolate and roasted chestnuts, should not be missed; they enhance the festive atmosphere. In busy places, stay mindful of your surroundings and watch out for your possessions. Explore well-known seasonal markets to find one-of-a-kind presents and mementos. Be

NYC CHRISTMAS

sure to get into the Christmas mood and enjoy everything that New York City has to offer at this wonderful time of the year. Visit famous sites like Rockefeller Center on your holiday journey in New York to see the enormous Christmas tree and go ice skating for a once-in-a-lifetime experience. Another must-see is Central Park, which is lit up for the holidays and provides a tranquil haven from the bustle of the city.

If you want to visit several sites at a price, think about purchasing a New York Pass. Additionally, seeing a Broadway production or a Christmas performance is a must-do NYC holiday tradition, so reserve your tickets beforehand. Bring with you a quality camera or smartphone with plenty of capacity so you will be able to capture the splendor of the city. And for a convenient experience, utilize apps for meal reservations, navigation, and finding local events. Finally, adopt a giving mindset by helping out at a local charity or volunteering. In addition to sightseeing, New York's holiday season

NYC CHRISTMAS

encourages sharing happiness and goodwill with those in need, making your trip even more meaningful.

NYC CHRISTMAS

Staying Safe in the Big Apple: Emergency Information for Your NYC Trip

It's crucial to understand how to be safe while having fun in New York City and who to contact in case of an emergency.

- In any life-threatening crisis, be it that it involves medicine, fire, or the police, dial 911 for quick help.

- You can dial 311 to get in touch with the NYPD (New York Police Department) for non-emergencies. Call 311 or go to an urgent care facility or hospital if you need medical assistance that is not an emergency.

- Contact the MTA (Metropolitan transit Authority) at 511 or go to their website if you misplace anything or need help using public transit.

NYC CHRISTMAS

Keep in mind that safety should always come first, and knowing who to call will help you relax and enjoy your stay in the busy metropolis of New York.

NYC CHRISTMAS

Your New York Christmas trip awaits in the center of the busy city, providing moments to treasure forever. As your trip through the glistening lights, joyous performances, and jubilant streets comes to an end, keep in mind the warmth and enchantment you experienced. New York is a city where hopes are rekindled and dreams come true, particularly during the holiday season. The holiday mood is embodied by the sight of the enormous Christmas tree at Rockefeller Center, the joy on the ice, and the love shared with family and friends.

Take with you the pleasure of the Christmas season, the giving spirit, and the warmth of the New York welcome as you say goodbye to this dynamic city. I hope the memories you've formed here serve as a constant reminder of the wonder of Christmas in the Big Apple. Happy Christmas and safe travels!

Made in the USA
Las Vegas, NV
11 November 2023